DONALD TRUMP

Meets His Maker

An Illustrated Play

DONALD TRUMP
Meets His Maker

An Illustrated Play

GABRIEL MIKAELIS CASSIDY

ARTWORK BY NICOLE ZAI

ARPress
45 Dan Road Suite 5
Canton MA 02021

Hotline: 1(888) 821-0229
Fax: 1(508) 545-7580

Ordering Information:

Quantity sales. Special discounts are available on quantity purchases by corporations, associations, and others. For details, contact the publisher at the address above.

Printed in the United States of America.

ISBN-13:   Softcover   979-8-89330-400-8
                eBook   979-8-89330-401-5

Library of Congress Control Number: 2024900502

I dedicate this play to my father, who died in the spring of 2023. He was a first-rate physician, in part because he habitually reserved judgment regarding his fellow human beings—until, that is, the ascendancy of Donald Trump, whom Dad hated with a passion. I dearly wish he were alive to read—or even better, see—this play.

In an email to Donald Trump's legal advisor John Eastman, Vice President Mike Pence's chief counsel Gregory Jacob wrote that Eastman's legal advice had functioned like "a serpent in the ear of the president of the United States."

In a response to Jacob's email, Eastman replied, "You know [Trump]—once he gets something in his head, it is hard to get him to change course."

Cast of characters, in order of appearance:

- **Donald Trump,** President of the United States

- **Anthony Ornato,** White House Deputy Chief of Staff for Operations

- **Cassidy Hutchinson**, executive assistant to Donald Trump's Chief of Staff Mark Meadows

- **Robert Engel,** head of the President's Secret Service Protective Detail

- **Walt Nauta**, President Donald Trump's Valet

- **Mark Meadows,** President Donald Trump's Chief of Staff

- **The Grim Reaper**

- **Satan**

- **Pat Cipollone,** White House Counsel

- **Ivanka Trump**, daughter of Donald Trump

Note to reader: If you would like to view the video clips referenced in this play, they are all contained in a single video that is accessible via the following URL: https://youtu.be/3A8KcCfon10?si=471bOI0VBB3GNiKs

Scene 1

Anthony Ornato,
White House Deputy Chief of Staff for Operations

Donald Trump, Anthony Ornato, and Cassidy Hutchinson stand on the stage at the Ellipse before Trump's January 6th oration. According to Hutchinson, Trump demanded that the metal detectors at the Ellipse's entrances be removed so that those of his followers who were armed could enter the grounds and thereby increase the size of the audience. A stunned Hutchinson looks on as the following exchange takes place between Trump and Ornato.

Trump (T): I want my audience for this historic moment to be huge, Tony. Why are so many of my people on the mall instead of here in front of me?

Anthony Ornato (Ornato): They don't want to come in, Mr. President. They have weapons that they don't want confiscated by the Secret Service. And they're fine on the mall. They can see you and they want to march straight to the Capitol from the mall.

T: I don't fucking care that they have weapons! They're not here to hurt me. Take the fucking metal detectors away! Let my people in! They can march to the Capitol from here.

Ornato: I'll see what I can do, sir.

Scene 2

President Trump speaking at the January 6th, 2021, rally.

On a gigantic screen at the back of the stage, a video is projected, containing an excerpt from Trump's galvanizing January 6th speech. The speech ran about 70 minutes, from around noon until 1:10 PM.

T: *[Speech excerpt. A video clip of the speech excerpt can be accessed via the following URL:* https://youtu.be/3A8KcCfon10?si=471bOI0VBB3GNiKs*]* "Now it is up to Congress to confront this egregious assault on our democracy. After this, we're going to walk down and I'll be there with you… We're going to walk down to the Capitol, and we're going to cheer on our brave Senators, and Congressmen and women. We're probably not going to be cheering so much for some of them because you'll never take back our country with weakness. You have to show strength, and you have to be strong."

Scene 3

Robert Engel,
Head of President Trump's Secret Service Protective Detail

This scene takes place in a presidential limousine—in this case, an SUV. According to Cassidy Hutchinson, an altercation took place pitting Trump against Robert Engel and Ornato about driving to the Capitol. Engel is in the driver's seat; Ornato is riding shotgun; Trump sits in the back seat.

T: To the Capitol! Step on it!

Ornato: I'm so sorry, sir, but we're returning to the White House.

T: I'm the fucking President! Take me to the Capitol!

Robert Engel (Engel): It will be too dangerous for you there, Mr. President. We have to go back to the West Wing.

T: *[Reaches for the steering wheel]* You sons of bitches!

Engel: *[Grabs Trump's arm]* Sir, you need to keep your hand off the steering wheel! We're going back to the West Wing. We're not going to the Capitol.

[With his free hand, Trump lunges towards Engel. Ornato grabs Trump by the wrist.]

Ornato: Please don't make me have to hurt you, Boss!

T: God damn it! You're hurting me already! Let go! That's an order!

Ornato: Aye aye, sir. *[Releases Trump's wrist. After a pause]* We'll head for the White House, Mr. President.

T: Fine! For now! I'll have a talk with both of you soon!

Scene 4

Donald Trump's Valet
Walt Nauta

This scene takes place in the White House, where Trump arrived at 1:21 PM, the time of the last entry in the Presidential Daily Diary till 4:03 PM. There were also no photographs taken of Trump between 1:21 and 4:00, and no phone calls recorded in the Presidential Call Log from 11:06 AM until 6:54 PM.

Walt Nauta (Nauta): Magnificent speech, Mr. President.

T: It was magnificent until after it ended. If anybody ever listened to me around here, I'd be at the Capitol right now.

[A brief silence ensues, which Nauta breaks.]

Nauta: Let me help you with your coat, sir. Speaking of the Capitol, there's a crowd of angry people there, Boss.

T: That's what I'm talking about. I want to watch my people rumble. Let's go to the dining room. *[They exit for the dining room.]*

Scene 5

*President Trump's supporters converging on the Capitol
after his January 6th speech*

This scene, and the remainder of the play, take place in the
private dining room just off the Oval Office.

Nauta: The usual channel, Mr. President?

T: *[Growling]* What do you think!? *[A pause, as the screen
at the back of the stage comes to life]* Will you look at that?
Those are some true patriots… Get me two Big Macs,
lots of fries, and a couple Diet Cokes.

Nauta: Right away, Boss.

*[Nauta exits and then returns, carrying four Diet Cokes on
a tray. He walks to where Trump is seated and places the*

Diet Cokes in can holders in the arms of Trump's easy chair.]

Nauta: Your burgers and fries will arrive shortly. Anything else, Mr. President?

T: Get Meadows in here. And give me the remote.

Nauta: Yes, sir! *[Hands the remote to Trump and exits]*

[After a brief period of time, during which Trump sits rivetted by what he—and the play's audience—see on the screen, there's a knock at the dining room door.]

T: Who is it?

Mark Meadows: It's Mark, sir. Can I come in, please?

T: I paged you, didn't I?

Meadows: *[Enters, meekly]* Powerful speech, Mr. President. And now, as predicted, there seems to be a problem at the Capitol, sir.

T: *[Waving in the direction of the television screen]* As you know, that's not a problem, you pissant. That's the solution. But damn it, Mark, I should be there with them. You said all was in order for me to go to the Capitol.

Meadows: Apparently the Secret Service didn't get the memo, Mr. President.

T: Bobby and Tony will be hearing from me soon. So will you, you can count on that. For now, make sure the limo is ready to go, in case Pence requires reinforcements. In the meantime, I want to be left alone, so I can watch my army in action. No phone calls. No photographs. No nothing! See to it. Now go!

Meadows: Yes, sir!

[As Meadows exits, Nauta pokes his head in through the door.]

Nauta: I have your lunch, Mr. President.

T: Great! I'm starving.

Nauta: *[Walks in and places all the food on a table sitting alongside Trump's easy chair]* I brought lots of napkins, too. May I do anything else for you, sir?

T: That will be all.

Nauta: Enjoy!

[Nauta exits, and Trump tucks into his meal, a show in itself. After about a minute, the Grim Reaper materializes out of smoke, explosions, etc.]

The Grim Reaper

T: God damn it, I said I want to be alone!

Grim Reaper (G): And so you are. Alone are all mortals in the end.

T: Oh, it's you, Grim! What brings you to Washington?

G: You and I have a date.

T: I'm sorry. You're not my type. *[Trump chuckles.]*

G: This is no laughing matter. And I don't have time to dilly dally. I have a full plate: places to go and people to meet.

T: I'm busy, too! You had your shot at me back in October when I had the China virus, but I survived, and now I have a protest to oversee. *[Points at the television screen]* Check it out.

G: Your mundane affairs are of no concern to me. I arrive when the time is ripe. And I <u>always</u> get my man.

T: But you've made a terrible mistake. I bet you're looking for my son. He has the same name as mine. Is it Donnie you've come for?

G: Ask not for whom Grim Reaper comes. I come for thee.

T: But I'm the wrong guy, I tell you! What about Biden? He's old as dirt, and he's a filthy, fucking cheater. He's your man!

G: His time will come soon enough. Your time is now.

T: That's a stinking lie.

G: Given the source, I'll take that as a compliment, for it means I speak the truth.

T: *[Bellows]* Give me a break! You come for me on this, the day of my greatest glory! *[Stands up, walks over to the television screen, and lifts his arm up, palm open, his fingers pointed at the screen]* I have thousands of supporters; any one of them will gladly stand in for me. Take your pick. What's mine is yours.

G: You always ever valued only your own life. I, however, am an equal opportunity destroyer. And I want you.

T: Who do you think you are, Uncle Sam? I'm warning you, I'll fight like hell!

G: You mean just as your lumpen Trumpkins do at the Capitol, even now? They fight like the hellbound, at least. You told them you'd be there with them. Well, you'll meet some of them up close and personal very soon. You'll be bosom buddies; it's tight quarters where you're headed, and toasty, too.

T: But I'm irreplaceable. Without me in the picture, this amazing day will be forgotten. You can't have me! I'll stop your steal!

G: You stop me!? Give _me_ a break! Do you suppose you're the first to try to defy death?

T: You've rigged this game like no one's ever rigged a game before.

G: This is no game! I don't play! I mean deadly, serious business.

T: But don't you see? This is dangerous for you. If I die suddenly, my base will be very suspicious. When word gets out that you made off with me, my followers will hunt you down. Do you think they'll stand for this? No!

President Trump's devotees breach the Capitol

G: Idle threats. And I don't cut deals; I cut straight to the chase. *[Runs his left hand along his scythe blade]*

T: Enough already! If you won't listen to me, talk to my lawyer.

[Trump returns to his chair and calls Rudy Giuliani.]

T: Hello, Rudy? It's the President…

G: *[Lifts his scythe as if ready to strike]* If you think I'm talking to your lunatic of a lawyer—

T: Just a minute, Rudy. *[Lowers the phone and places his hand over its mouthpiece]* Easy, Grim. I take your point. Just let me sign off with him. *[Trump stands and puts some distance between Grim and himself.]* I'm back, Rudy.

Giuliani: . . .

T: Yes, I can see what's happening.

Giuliani: . . .

T: Yes, I know what the plan was. I couldn't get a fucking ride to the Capitol, all right? Engel and Ornato failed me, so I'm stuck here in the White House. *[Lowers his voice to a loud whisper]* I've got another urgent problem on my hands. The fucking Grim Reaper's here in the dining room.

Giuliani: . . .

T: This is no shit, Rudy. Scythe and all. I told him I can't die at a time like this, but he's bound and determined to take me out. Got any strokes of genius?

Giuliani: . . .

T: Good idea! You're my kind of lawyer; I don't care what they say. Bye.

G: Is that a flipphone?

T: It's called a burner phone, buddy, a term Satan would get a kick out of. Speaking of which, I'd like to talk with Satan about all this.

G: *[Deadpan]* The devil you say.

T: *[A pause, during which Trump glares at Grim]* You told me this is no laughing matter.

G: *[Mocking remorse]* Do forgive me! I just couldn't resist.

T: To repeat: I want to see our manager.

G: What business do you have with him?

T: Satan's the man! If anyone can spare my life, he can.

G: For your information, Satan dispatched me here, in order to collect your debt.

T: But why?

G: You've exhausted his patience, it would seem. He said, and I quote, "Today is the final straw."

T: How can that be? I'm doing Satan's work up here. *[Nods in the direction of the television screen]*

G: He said, and I quote, "Too many wasted opportunities."

T: What!? There may have been a hiccup or two along the way, but I've remained absolutely faithful to him and the mission since I became president. That has to count for something. I only need a second chance—and better yet, a second term. I'll make the most of it, believe me.

G: Satan offers but one deal per customer. You made yours some time back.

T: All I want is one meeting. I've learned a lot from Satan over the years, but now I may have a thing or two to teach him.

G: And what would you teach your mentor, do tell?

T: First, loyalty is all-important. If you don't bring that to the table, you don't get a seat.

[Pregnant pause, during which Trump smiles broadly]

G: *[Sarcastically]* What an insight. And your second revelation?

T: The art of the pardon.

G: I see. And what do these pearls of wisdom have to do with the matter at hand?

T: Well, let's take for example three pardons I issued, to Michael Flynn, Paul Manafort, and Robert Stone. They may have made some mistakes, but they remained loyal to me, and now they're free, thanks to yours truly. Then there's my case. Let's say for the sake of argument that I didn't take full advantage of a couple opportunities. I'm <u>still</u> the most loyal disciple that Satan will ever have. I should be rewarded.

G: And how would you have Satan reward your <u>incomparable</u> loyalty?

T: He should exercise his awesome power and pardon me.

G: You do know that forgiveness is not Satan's long suit, right?

T: I can be very con-vincing.

G: *[Sighs]* Oh, all right. My master is your master, and this may just be a special case. You are a very valued servant. I suppose it can't hurt if you talk with him. You know the incantation: Call upon him as you have in the past.

T: *[Clicks his heels together three times, while intoning]* Hail, Satan, full of hate. Hail, Satan, full of hate. Hail, Satan, full of hate.

[Satan materializes out of smoke, explosions, etc.]

Satan

Satan (S): You rang?

T: Your stooge here claims my number's up.

S: So I've heard. I must say I'm disappointed to find you here, Donald. You're supposed to be at the Capitol.

T: Engel and Ornato refused to drive me there. I tried strongarming Bobby, but he wouldn't cooperate with me. I thought you had the Secret Service under your thumb. Where were you when I needed you?

S: I don't have free rein up here, Donald, my boy. God occasionally intervenes, and he works in strange ways.

Today, Bobby and Tony answered to their so-called better angels.

T: I understand. I'm the fucking president, and I still don't always get my way. I read them the riot act. Nothing doing. You can't hold that against me.

S: You can't find good help anymore, it would seem. *[Pregnant pause]* As you'll recall, you and I made a deal: The presidency for your soul. I held up my end, and I must say you've held up yours. You've created laudable chaos while in office. Aiding and abetting the pandemic was genius. Now that you are out of power, though, you're of no further use to me.

T: But I have so much more havoc I can wreak. Feast your eyes on the spectacle unfolding on the screen. *[Trump beams at the television screen on the wall. After a pause]* All my doing.

S: If you want to stay out of prison, you'd best not go trumpeting your leading role in this bedlam. You're no good to anyone in jail. Remember, plausible deniability. Say it after me: plau-si-ble de-ni-a-bil-i-ty.

T: *[Dismissively]* Plausible deniability. I get it. And now get this: I'm no good to anyone <u>dead,</u> either.

S: I'll be the judge of that.

[Trump's phone rings.]

T: It's Rudy. I'll make it snappy.

S: Tell him I say hello.

[Trump answers his phone. During the call, Satan and Grim have their eyes on the screen.]

T: Hi, Rudy.

Giuliani: . . .

T: Satan's here. He says hello.

Giuliani: . . .

T: I'll give it my best shot. We'll see what happens. Gotta go. *[Hangs up and turns to Satan]* Rudy says hello back at you.

S: He's a gentleman, if not a scholar. While you were on the phone, I was taking in the show. *[Nods at the screen]* Very impressive, Donald. It's pandemonium out there. You've unleashed an unholy horde.

T: There's never been a movement like it. And all for me. Did you hear them today during my speech? "We love Trump! We love Trump! We love Trump!" they chanted.

S: Even so, Grim here is my right-hand man. He has a perfect track record.

T: But you can overrule him, can't you? You're his boss, as well as mine. Hear me out. I'll make a case for keeping me alive. I reviewed some of my accomplishments with the throng at the rally today. Please allow me to remind you of just a handful of the many special memories we share from the last few years.

S: If you insissst.

T: I call this Trump's Top Ten.

S: Very nice: Alliteration. But I prefer asssonance. Let's make it sssixxx, my favorite number.

T: It's your losss.   Trump's Big Six it is. *[Points the remote at the screen and brings up a video, which begins to play.]* Number sssixxx!

Intermission

Scene 6

A good part of this scene is given over to the president's presentation of Trump's Big Six.   If the reader would like to view the video clips that President Trump plays for Satan, they are all contained in a single video that can be accessed via the following URL:

https://youtu.be/3A8KcCfon10?si=471bOI0VBB3GNiKs

T: Number sssixxx! *[Trump starts video.]*

6) Trump's announcement of his candidacy for president, at Trump Tower in New York City; June 16ᵗʰ, 2015: "When Mexico sends its people, they're not sending their best. They're not sending you. *[Points at someone in the audience]* They're not sending you. *[Points at someone else in the audience]* They're sending people that have lots of problems, and they're bringing those problems with us. They're bringing drugs. They're bringing crime. They're rapists."

[Trump stops video.]

S: A trip down Memory Lane. You did announce your candidacy for president with your customary flair. Poor Mexico: America's longstanding whipping boy. In point of fact, though, <u>you</u> are a rapist.

T: Are you referring to my "grab them by the pussy" remark? *[Chortles]* After that video went viral, I explained that it was just a case of locker room banter, but in fact, that was my modus operandi with women. And sometimes it worked! I tell you this because you of course know the truth.

S: *[Breaks into a little song and dance]* I know when you've been bad or good, So be bad for badness' sake. *[Laughs gleefully]*

T: You think rape is badass, try this on for size. Number 5! I give you the showstopper from my 2016 Republican

Convention speech. *[Trump starts video. A video clip of this speech excerpt that President Trump shows Satan can be accessed via the following URL:* https://youtu.be/3A8KcCfon10?si=471bOI0VBB3GNiKs*]*

Donald Trump during his speech on July 21, the last day of the 2016 Republican Presidential Convention

5) Republican Convention speech in Cleveland, Ohio; July 21ˢᵗ, 2016: "Nobody knows the system better than me… which is why I alone can fix it."

[Trump stops video.]

T: And I alone am fixing it—the election, I mean. Look! *[Trump, Satan, and Grim stare at the television screen for a good minute.]* My minions have broken into the Capitol! We'll right this wrong yet.

S: As you often say, we'll see what happens. Sometimes might <u>does</u> make right. At a price, though, Donald, witness the American carnage taking place in the Capitol before our eyes.

T: Come on, Satan. Don't tell me you have a problem with that? *[Trump, Satan, and Grim share a laugh.]* Besides, a guy can't make good on <u>all</u> his campaign promises. And this American carnage is in the name of truth and justice.

[Knock, knock]

T: Now who is it!?

Meadows: I'm so sorry. It's Pat and Mark, sir. May we have just a minute of your time, please?

T: *[To Satan and Grim]* Make yourselves scarce.

S: We'll move into the corner. But not to worry. Only he we come for can see us.

T: Good to know. *[Pauses while Satan and Grim walk to the corner, and then turns towards the dining room door]* You may enter.

[The door opens, and Meadows and Pat Cipollone enter.]

Pat Cipollone, White House Counsel

Pat Cipollone (Cipollone): You must put out a statement <u>now</u>, Mr. President! The crowd is calling for Pence's head, for God's sake!

T: What am I going to say, Pat? They're doing nothing wrong! And Mike deserves it.

Cipollone: The election is <u>over</u>, sir. And if Mike is killed, it will be on you.

T: I'm good with that. Mike could have been a hero. Now he's the GOAT: The Greatest-of-All-Time Loser.

Cipollone: More like the scapegoat.

T: Shut the fuck up, Pat! Mark, I told you I want to be alone! Be gone, both of you, before I get really mad!

[Meadows and Cipollone scurry for the door.]

Cipollone: *[Under his breath, to Meadows]* He's mad, all right.

T: Why, youuu! *[Rushes towards Meadows and Cipollone. They bolt out of the door and slam it.]* And don't come back! *[Trump laughs with amusement.]*

[Satan and Grim come out of the shadows.]

T: Thank you for your patience, gentlemen. Before I continue, just one more brief pause, while I fan the flames.

[Trump composes a Tweet on the television screen.] *"Mike Pence didn't have the courage to do what should have been done to protect our Country and our Constitution, giving States a chance to certify a corrected set of facts, not the fraudulent or inaccurate ones which they were asked to previously certify. USA demands the truth!"*

[Trump posts the Tweet.]

Gallows erected by President Trump followers outside the Capitol

T: That should stir the pot.

S: Bravo! <u>Now</u> you're showing some backbone.

T: *[Glares at Satan]* Once the real people have triumphed and I'm back in power, I'll show even more backbone than I have so far. For instance, I'll bring back family separation. Number 4! *[Trump starts video. A video clip of this speech excerpt that President Trump shows Satan can be accessed via the following URL:*

https://youtu.be/3A8KcCfon10?si=471bOI0VBB3 GNiKs*]*

4) Jeff Sessions' announcement of the Zero Tolerance Policy; May 8th, 2018: "If you are smuggling a child, then we're going to prosecute you, and that child will be separated from you, probably, as required by law. If you don't want your child separated, then don't bring him across the border illegally."

[Trump stops video.]

S: Jeff Sessions! Long time no see! Kate McKinnon nailed him on *Saturday Night Live*. He is a weasel. Which is a good thing!

T: He betrayed me on Russia, but he was balls to the wall on immigration. And thank you for connecting me with Stephen Miller. Family separation was really his baby. *[Still photo of Miller flashes on the screen; Trump chuckles.]* He not only looks evil; he is evil.

Stephen Miller,
White House Director of Speechwriting to President Donald Trump

S: A man after our own hearts. But just two months after Zero Tolerance became official policy, you cancelled it with an executive order. Why? Was it too heartless for even you?

T: *[Snorts]* For me? No chance. But it was for Ivanka and Melania. They wouldn't stop bitching and moaning about all the wailing children.

S: You caved to a couple women?

T: You know me better than that. It was John Kelly who talked me out of it. He showed me some of the videos that everybody was watching.

S: *[Slowly and softly]* So it was the optics.

T: It did look terrible. A lot of people were upset. But I wish I hadn't called it off. That showed weakness. If I'd ridden it out, my base would have rallied around it. It was just a bunch of brown babies from shithole countries. I've pushed for the revival of family separation the last few months. *[Pounds his chest with his right fist while pointing at the screen with his left index finger]* When we've stopped the steal and I resume my rightful place as President, America's borders will be safe! Zero tolerance will be the order of the day!

[Knock,   knock]

T: Now what?

Ivanka Trump (Ivanka): It's Ivanka, Daddy. And Mark and Pat. May we come in, please?

Trump and his daughter Ivanka Trump on the stage at the Republican National Convention July 21, 2016

T: Just a moment. *[Looks at Satan and Grim and motions to the corner that they retreated to during the previous visit by Meadows and Cipollone. Trump then turns towards the dining room door.]* Come in. *[Ivanka, Meadows, and Cipollone enter and approach Trump.]* What do you want?

Cipollone: The whole nation is watching America burn and sees you doing nothing to stop it, sir.

Ivanka: You want everyone to know you care, Dad. We've written a Tweet that will show that.

T: Let me read it. *[Ivanka hands Trump the handwritten message, which Trump reads out loud.]* "Please support our Capitol Police and Law Enforcement. They are truly on the side of our Country. Stand down!" Those last two words have got to go.

Cipollone: How about replacing them with, "Evacuate the Capitol?"

T: No, no, no!

Meadows: *[Softly]* "Please evacuate the Capitol?"

T: That's the same damn thing that Pat just said! And it's one too many pleases.

Ivanka: What do you think of, "Stay peaceful?"

T: *[Pregnant pause]* I can live with that. Now everybody out! You can post it after you've left.

Ivanka: Thank you, Daddy. *[Kisses Trump on the cheek]*

Meadows: Thank you, Mr. President.

Cipollone: Thank you, sir.

[Ivanka, Meadows, and Cipollone exit. Satan and Grim rejoin Trump.]

S: You're like silly putty in Ivanka's hands. She purrs sweet nothings in your ear, and you go squishy.

T: Hold on just a second. What's so squishy about "stay peaceful," Satan? *[Points at the screen]* Do <u>they</u> look "peaceful?" *[Pauses]* So "stay peaceful" is bullshit, right? It's good for one thing, though. Plausible deniability. Say it after me: plausible deniability.

S: Touche. Go on with your show.

T: Number 3! *[Trump starts video. A video clip of this speech excerpt that President Trump shows Satan can be accessed via the following URL:* https://youtu.be/3A8KcCfon10?si=471bOI0VBB3GNiKs*]*

President Trump and Vladimir Putin at the 2018 Helsinki Summit

3) Putin-Trump press conference in Helsinki; July 16th, 2018: "My people came to me, Dan Coats came to me and some others and said they think it's Russia. I have President Putin. He just said it's not Russia. I will say this. I don't see any reason why it would be."

[Trump stops video.]

T: Russian interference in the election?   What Russian interference in the election?   *[Trump and Satan cackle.]*   Need I show more?   You forgot how faithfully I've served you, didn't you?

S: So you have.   And so has Vlad.   He can lie with the best of them.

T: *[Jumps up and bustles over to a mirror on the wall]* Master, master of them all / Who's the falsest of them all? *[Turns and faces Satan]* Please! No one lies like I lie.

S: The shamelessness I armored you with facilitates the unblinking lie. But there's a <u>big</u> difference between Vlad and you. You've already mentioned your wishy washiness regarding family separation. Putin is <u>never</u> wishy washy. He gets things done. Look at what happened when you asked Russia to find those 30,000 missing Clinton emails. Presto!   They   magically   appeared. And   how?   Putin authorized their release, that's how. And what did you do to return the favor?   The Zelensky call.

T: A perfect call!   The full transcript of that phone call is top secret, but I'll share it with you, of course.

S: There's no need.   I remember it well.   *[Imploringly]* "So what are we going to do here, folks? I only need 11,000 votes." Ooops! Wrong "perfect call."   Let me try again.

[Venomously] "I would like you to do us a favor, though." *[Sneeringly]* Perfect call! That call was a textbook shakedown. It was like a scene out of *The Godfather*, except the Godfather doesn't just try; he succeeds. You tried to extort Zelensky, but he refused to buckle. The world will soon see how desperately Ukraine needs the weaponry you threatened to withhold. So much for your *[Makes air quotes with his hands]* "perfect call!" It is Exhibit A of your ineptitude. Ukraine got the weapons, you got nothing on Biden's son, and you nearly got impeached.

T: But I beat that impeachment. I've faced persecution the likes of which no president has ever seen. The Deep State can't catch me, though. I've outwitted its every witch hunt.

S: Technically, those would be warlock hunts.

T: I may be a sex fiend, but I'm no warlock. *[Laughs manically]* Anywaysss… I may have let you down once or twice, but I've learned my lesson. When I am president again, I'll surround myself with loyal, competent, ruthless people. They'll execute our every wish.

S: That's the watchword: Execution!

T: It's one of my favorite words! Number 2! When some governors tried to shut down their states in response to the pandemic, I weighed in with a barrage of Tweets. *[Trump projects three Tweets on the screen.]*

*2)   **Three   Tweets;   April   17th,   2020:***
"LIBERATE MINNESOTA!"; "LIBERATE MICHIGAN!"; "LIBERATE VIRGINIA, and save your great 2nd Amendment. It is under siege!"

T: Many great patriots answered my call. *[Trump starts video. On the screen is projected a video of protestors in and around the Lansing, Michigan, capitol building on April 30th, 2020. The video clip that President Trump shows Satan can be accessed via the following URL:* https://youtu.be/3A8KcCfon10?si=471bOI0VBB3GNiKs*]*

[Trump stops video.]

Protesters out front of the Lansing, Michigan, Capitol

S: Brilliant! That's one moment you got right. In the face of COVID-19, any past president would have called for national unity. Instead, you sowed discord, exhorting your acolytes to protest lockdowns. And that's just what they did, many of them armed, in Michigan.

T: A dress rehearsal for <u>this</u> beautiful protest, and that Tweet previewed my Tweet that set the stage for today. *[Projects Tweet on screen]* "*Big protest in D.C. on January 6th. Be there, will be wild!*"

S: You wily fox. There <u>is</u> a method to your madness.

T: By the way, some of my Proud Boys got their feet wet in Michigan. That skirmish primed them for more. Ever since, they've been loaded for bear. Standing by, as I commanded them in my debate with Sleepy Joe. *[Chuckles]*

S: You were on fire that night! Biden and Wallace couldn't get a word in edgewise. And the Proud Boys heard you, loud and clear. They've stood up today.

T: *[Gazing at the screen, which has cut back to images of the besieged Capitol, Trump extends his right arm and, with his lips pursed, gives a thumbs-up.]* What a team we are! I am the commander-in-chief of today's battle, and the Proud Boys are my shock troops. Such obedience is a sight to behold, and that mayhem is my wet dream, come true.

S: It's wild out there, all right.

T: This is the climax of the last four years! *[Punctuates his point with a pelvic thrust]*

[Trump's phone rings.]

T: *[Walks to his chair and looks at the caller ID on his phone]* Damn it! This is a call I have to take. *[Sits down and answers phone]* Hello, Kevin.

California Republican Congressman Kevin McCarthy

Kevin McCarthy (McCarthy): . . .

T: Those aren't my people. Those are—those are Antifa.

McCarthy: . . .

T: Well, Kevin, I guess they're just more upset about the election theft than you are.

McCarthy: . . .

T: Go fuck yourself! *[Trump hangs up.]* Jesus! Now there's someone with no backbone! *[Trump shakes his head.]* Where were we when we were so rudely interrupted? Ah, yes. Number 1! *[Trump projects a March 20th, 2020 Tweet on the screen.]*

> **1) The pandemic:** *"We have a perfectly coordinated and fine-tuned plan at the White House for our attack on CoronaVirus."*

[Trump clicks the remote and Fox News' coverage of the Capitol invasion returns to the screen.]

G: *[Grim makes air quotes with his hands.]* A perfect plan, for <u>me</u>. *[Smiles]* Thanks in part to your unbelievable response to the pandemic, over 340,000 Americans are dead, and counting. I've enjoyed a bumper crop this past year--a lot of them anti-vaxxers, of course, and big fans of yours. While it's invisible to you, I can see their blood on your hands; even Clorox won't rid you of those spots. My comrade in arms, I'm grateful to you thousands of times over. What execution!

[Trump bows.]

President Trump hosts a Pandemic Response Team Press Conference, with White House Coronavirus Response Coordinator Deborah Birx in the background

S: An entertaining argument, Donald. And the coronavirus whopper makes for a heartwarming conclusion to your highlight reel. Credit where credit's due: You were good for Grim's business. As it turned out, though, your COVID-19 misinformation machine proved your undoing. It's just possible that if more of your supporters had survived, they would have swung the election your way. In any event, given the death toll on your watch, it's no surprise 80 million people voted for Biden.

T: There's no way Biden got 80 million votes!

S: Tell it to the judges. I'll tell you this: You're no longer in a position to downplay the pandemic. Biden will be president in two weeks.

T: *[Points at the television screen]* Not if that mob has anything to say about it. They're fighting like hell, just like I told them!

S: All 250,000 of them? *[Chuckles]* Your presidency ends as it began, with an inflation of your audience numbers.

T: Alternative facts! Good old Kellyanne. The press went ballistic. They just couldn't believe we'd lie like that, and right out of the gate, about something like the size of the Inaugural audience. Well, I've lied non-stop ever since. In that, you are my role model, O Great Deceiver.

S: Alas, my dear Donald, it's all been for naught. When the Secret Service defied your order to drive you to the Capitol, the die was cast. Without you there to lead them on, your rabid host will be repelled. Our cause is lost. The <u>Big</u> Lie is dead.

T: Big Lie? What Big Lie?

A Big Lie believer

S: Your claim that you won the election, you ninny!

T: But that's no lie! It's the truth! Thought you could deceive <u>me</u>, did you, Satan?

S: *[Sneeringly]* What? You <u>believe</u> your own bilge?

T: You're just like all the other naysayers, Mr. Know-It-All.

S: With one big difference. This naysayer can see the future.

T: I'm not talking about the future; I'm talking about the past. The election was fraudulent! Biden's 80 million votes is a hoax. You probably don't follow social media the way I do, Satan. The evidence is all over the internet.

S: Evidence of voter fraud? Go on! You saw how persuasive your evidence was in court. Your henchman Giuliani and his ilk brought over sixty cases, and all but one was unsuccessful. You may be the executive branch, Mr. President, but you get a big, fat zero for execution on that one. Even judges you appointed dismissed your lawyers' arguments, for crying out loud.

T: That's the swamp of the Deep State for you. It sucks in all who enter it.

S: And your water boy Billy Barr? He called it all baloney, too.

T: Barr's a traitor! He's not only disloyal; he's ungrateful. I made him. Without me, he'd be a nobody, and that's what he is to me now.

G: You leave Bill Barr to me. I'll see him soon enough, right, Boss?

S: *[Pats Grim on the back]* So you will, Grim, so you will. *[Turns back to Trump]* You see, Donald, I prize loyalty, too. When you allowed the Secret Service to overrule you and drive you here instead of the Capitol, you foiled our plan. That's why I dispatched Grim your way.

G: Told you I'm never wrong! Trumpy, Trumpy, sat on a

wall/Trumpy, Trumpy, had a great fall-- *[Raises his scythe]*

S: Now, now, Grim. Hold your hand. This may be a special case, after all. So you think you won the election, Donald?

T: In a landslide! The only way I lost is if it was rigged.

S: A true believer, hmmm?

[Knock, knock]

T: Holy shit! Now what?

Meadows: It's Mark again, Mr. President. Just one more little interruption, if you please?

T: This is the last time! *[Nods to Satan and Grim to retreat back to the corner of the room again. Satan puts his right arm around Grim's shoulder and guides him in that direction.]*

G: *[As Satan and Grim walk, whispers to Satan]* Maybe he's told that lie so many times he believes it himself, master.

S: *[Holds index finger to his lips. In a soft, sibilant voice]* Ssshhh. Leave this to me, my boy.

T: *[Turns towards the dining room door]* This better be good, Mark.

Meadows: *[Opens the door and remains standing at the threshold as he speaks]* I'm sorry to disturb you, Mr. President, but law enforcement's getting trampled. It's a bad look.

T: Fine! Send out another Tweet in my name. Tell the crowd to go easy on the police. No mercy for Pence or Pelosi, though.

Meadows: Got it!

T: Now scram! And don't come back.

Meadows: Yes, sir! *[Closes the door]*

President Trump's Chief of Staff Mark Meadows

[Satan and Grim rejoin Trump at the dining room table.]

T: You were saying?

S: Unfortunately, today is lost. However, you'll live to fight—like hell, I presume—another day.

T: *[Gloats at Grim]* I knew he'd see things my way.

G: Don't you dare strut, Trump. It's but a reprieve.

S: I'll not only spare you, Donald; I'll provide you with a plan of action. You must send out two very important messages today. I'll help you write them.

T: I get it. A ghost writer.

S: *[Gives Trump a double take]* Aren't you the clever one? Now let me take the wheel. *[Satan and Trump switch seats, and Satan begins typing.]* "I know your pain. I know you're hurt. We had an election that was stolen from us."*

T: That's right!

"It was a landslide election, and everyone knows it, especially the other side."

T: Bingo!

Satan: Pipe down! I can hardly hear myself think! *[Satan resumes typing.]* "But you have to go home now. We have to have peace. We have to have law and order. We have to respect our great people in law and order. We don't want anybody hurt. It's a very tough* *period of time. There's never been a time like this where such a thing happened, where they could take it away from all of us, from me, from you, from our country. This was a fraudulent election, but we can't play into the hands of these people. We have to have peace. So go home."*

S: Hot off the press!   *[Holds his finger to his rear end]* Sssss!

T: Wow! You type like the wind. And it sounds just like me. Can I add some words, though?

S: If you insissst.

[Trump and Satan switch places, and Trump types.]

"We love you. You're very special. You've seen what happens. You see the way others are treated that are so bad and so evil. I know how you feel, but go home and go home in peace."

T: There. What do you think?

S: I don't know what the next-to-last sentence means, but thanks to the word "evil," I'm all for it.   *[Satan and Trump share a belly laugh.]* All right; it's a wrap. Put that out in a video, not a Tweet, around 4:00. It should pacify Ivanka and your toadies.

An image taken from President Trump's "We love you" video, recorded at 4:03 PM and released at 4:17 PM on January 6th

S: Now for the second message. Gangway. *[Trump and Satan switch places at the console again.]* This one's for your foot soldiers.   Have to throw the seals some fishesss. *[Satan begins typing.]*

"These are the things and events that happen when a sacred landslide election victory . . ."

T: "Sacred?" I love it, but really? Seems a bit over the top, especially coming from you.

S: *[Looks up and smiles]* Gotta cover my tracks. *[Continues typing]* "is so unceremoniously & viciously stripped away. . ."

T: "Unceremoniously!" That's beautiful. But did you spell it right?

[Satan casts Trump a withering glance.]

T: *[Whimpering]* Don't you at least want to capitalize it?

S: Oh, do shut up! *[Continues typing]* "from great patriots who have been badly & unfairly treated for so long." That should clean up the mess of a sentence you wrote for the previous Tweet.

T: Riiight.

[Satan continues typing.] "Go home with love & in peace. Thank you."

T: Ohhh, yes! They do love me so! But wait. It needs to end with a bang. Let me take a crack at it.

S: Knock yourself out.

[Trump and Satan switch places again. Trump deletes "Thank you" and then types.] "God bless you, and God bless America."

S: Over my dead body. I'm all for tongue in cheek, but that's just disgusting. Worse yet, it's trite.

T: My bad. I'll save it for another Tweet.

S: I swear. I have to do everything around here. Move over! *[Satan displaces Trump and types.]* *"Remember this day forever!"* There!

T: Perfect! *[Puts his right hand's three middle fingers and thumb to his mouth and kisses them]* Forever and ever and ever.

S: You see, we want your people to believe their efforts were justified, historic, and appreciated. We'll require their blind allegiance again for future American carnage.

T: Now you're talking.

S: Post that around 6:00 tonight.

T: Will do.

S: And henceforth—forever and ever and ever—make that your mantra. This election was stolen. You and your people were robbed. Biden president? A hoax, all thanks to the radical left Democrats and the fake news media.

T: That's what I've been saying all along.

S: And keep saying it. The more you repeat it, the more your base will buy into it. You've cocked the trigger. It's yours to keep it cocked.

T: But when can I pull the trigger again?

S: In good time, my pretty, in good time.

Grim: *[Forlornly]* What about me?

S: Relax, Grim. You'll meet your quota for the day in the Capitol: Two heart attacks, one drug overdose, and one shooting. Keep up the good work.

Grim: At your service, Satan. *[Grim bows.]*

T: So I'm off the hook?

S: *[Pregnant pause as Satan glances at Grim's scythe]* You're on probation, Donald. But don't fail me again.

T: You can count on me. I'm ever your obedient servant.

S: You owe me your soul, and then some. Off I go. I've got other fish to fry. *[Hoots with laughter]* Remember: Your show must go on.

T: I'm the greatest show on earth. And there's a sucker born every minute.

S: You've got fish to fry too, then. *[Satan and Trump laugh diabolically together.]* Don't forget those two messages. And tomorrow send something out that creates the appearance of contrition.

T: Thy will be done.

S and G: *[Simultaneously, in harmony, to the tune of "Happy Trails"] Until we meet again. [Satan and Grim disappear in a cloud of smoke.]*

T: *[A pregnant pause, while the smoke clears]* I <u>am</u> the falsest of them all. I can con even Satan. And sometimes, I con even myself. *[Looks out at the audience with the same facial gestures and body language Trump employed after the line, "Nobody knows the system better than me,"during his 2016 Republican Convention speech. Then the lights go dark.]*

Donald Trump during his speech on July 21, the last day of the 2016 Republican Presidential Convention

ACKNOWLEDGMENTS

Because there are countless people I could acknowledge, most will go unnamed; a handful I will identify by initials. First, thanks go out to all those who read and responded to the various drafts of the play; you know who you are. Special thanks go out to MD and LM, without whose encouragement I may have ceased working on the play, and to JS, who impressed upon me the importance that the play be, if not mounted on stage, at least available in book form during the presidential election year ahead. One individual I will acknowledge by name is Cassidy Hutchinson; this play is informed by her highly credible public testimony before the House Select Committee to Investigate the January 6th Attack on the U.S. Capitol.

Thanks also to my son, who created the URL via which readers can view the video clips referenced in the play; he also introduced me to the artist whose illustrations grace this book and its cover. My gratitude to my wife, too; she prodded me to do the due diligence that resulted both in my finding a publisher of integrity, and in this book being illustrated. Finally, I am grateful that so many people near and dear to me share my deep-seated belief in democracy.

9 798889 330400 8